# From NO Where
# To NOW Here

Maurice Blair

Katrina'sWORKS
P U B L I S H I N G

No part of this book may be used or reproduced in
any matter without permission, except in the case of
brief quotations embodied in articles or reviews.
Models used for cover and trailer were acquired from
canstockphoto.com
All rights are reserved by the author.

ISBN-978-0692677094
ISBN-0692677097
**From NO Where To NOW Here**

**Copyright © March 2016
Maurice Blair**

**Edited by Katrina Avant
Cover Design
Soul Sister Ink**

**K a t r i n a s w o r k s . c o m**

## Dedication

This book is dedicated to the people I've met during my lifetime, who have opened my eyes to life and its greatness. To my dad, Freddie Steward, who started me in the career of trucking and spent time showing me the way of the road. To my mother, Sarah Blair and stepdad, George Blair, who raised me and instilled the importance of hard work and integrity. To my grandmother, Elmer Amos, who taught me the importance of being kind and respectful to all people. To my loving wife, Jackie Blair, who has endured and embraced the hardships of life with me. To my adoring children, sisters, brothers, family, friends and everyone who has believed in me and helped me along the journey of life....Thank You!

# Contents

Foreword ..................................................................... 1
Introduction .................................................................. 3
Life's Seven Basic Mile Markers ........................................ 6
    Life Mile Marker 118: Greatness ............................... 7
    Life Mile Marker 128: Words ..................................... 9
    Life Mile Marker 138: Love ...................................... 11
    Life Mile Marker 148: The Process ........................... 13
    Life Mile Marker 158: Suffering ................................ 15
    Life Mile Marker 168: Longevity .............................. 18
    Life Mile Marker 178: Reality ................................... 20
More Mile Markers for Life ............................................ 22
    Greatness ............................................................. 29
    Words ................................................................... 31
    Love ..................................................................... 34
    The Process ......................................................... 38
    Suffering .............................................................. 42
    Longevity ............................................................. 48
    Reality .................................................................. 55
    Conclusion: Success ............................................. 58
Notes ~~~ Looking at some of *Maurice's Mile Markers of Life* below, reflect on them and write down what they may mean for you. ............................................................ 60
Notes~~~ ................................................................... 63

# Foreword

Success means different things to different people. For some, it's power. For others, it's the respect of their peers, or it is self satisfaction. For many, it's the desire to have better relationships with the people in their lives.

Everyone wants to succeed, no question about that. Even people who are the most cynical and pessimistic want success. We all want to be more productive. We all want to feel as though we are controlling our destiny, that we are not controlled by it.

Maurice Blair has approached this book with a simplistic outline for success. His experiences serve as a moving example of what can happen when people care about others. Drawing from his experiences, as a long haul truck driver, to competing in the sport of body building, to working with students and parents in the West Memphis School District as a connection specialist, truancy officer, and mentor, Blair's actions and behaviors are rooted in more than three decades of experience as a working adult with success, with failure, and with learning how people's commitment—including his own—makes the difference.

Of the lessons Maurice shares, the mile marker of love is the most inspirational. Love is not always easy. As he shares, sometimes life requires tough love. Regardless of the time or circumstance, love is always rewarding. What a simple but so important life lesson.

This is a book that really challenges your life's perspective from two views: reflection and action. At the end of each day, we all get a chance to reflect on our choices and circumstances. The great thing about tomorrow is that we get to act on what is next. I think that is what we all are aiming for.

*From No Where To Now Here* speaks from every page. It is an inspiring read that is thoughtful and reassuring.

                        Jon Collins
                        Superintendent
                        West Memphis School District

## Introduction

Nothing is more humbling than thinking you have something to say about your life that may have meaning for someone else or encourage another person. As Langston Hughes, the great African-American poet would say, "Life for me ain't been no crystal stair." But then, it's all about perspective. It's not as if my life is such a profound or unique success story, in fact there was a time that I could not even see any success in it at all! Again, it is all about perspective. My life, like yours, is really all about Grace, Mercy and Hope. Grace, Mercy and Hope is what we all require to live the life tailor made for our own unique blessings and lessons. We live in a rapidly changing world where poverty is growing and the middle class is shrinking. Every day I observe young people struggling to find purpose and losing the fight too many times in search of purpose. They are not like the generations of parents who value work, education and family.

When I started this little book I just wanted to write about the things I get so excited about when making motivational speeches, talking to youth and adults and doing the community work which I love so much. Over the years as a professional driver, I audio recorded my thoughts or wrote them down. This gave me a great portion of my life experience to write this book. It also, allowed me to really appreciate and come to grips with my past. I used to think of my seventeen years on the road as a part of my life that I had struggled through and barely survived. I was grateful that I learned to be a body builder and a decent driver. I made many friends and took care of my family. But I also spent a lot of time wishing that I had done more, better and bigger with my life.

Then, one day, a friend asked me, "Where do you think you learned all that stuff that you talk about and that makes you the person you are? Who else would you be, really?" That question led me to make my years as a trucker the centerpiece of this book. Those years of struggle and alone time forced me to educate myself in an uncommon way, to go from being the shyest person I've ever seen to having limitless curiosity and the courage to talk to anybody, anytime, anywhere! It sent me to the libraries and bookstores in cities where people who looked like me were not often seen. I was a country boy from Greenville, Mississippi who started out with a limited vocabulary that I felt desperate to enlarge.

Getting stranded in an out of the way town in North Dakota as the only African-American man in that town, taught me the power of a smile, courage and to genuinely accept others where they stand. I learned how to eat sparingly when I ran low on money on the road; how to survive a few nights in jail for an unpaid violation made by the trucking company I was driving for, which was never paid to that state; how to take the hard rousing from other drivers, because I chose not to take advantage of the truck stop "ladies"; and how to discipline myself and stay healthy.

I learned to look for a gym and exercise on every lay over and to eat healthy. This led to a sidebar career as a body builder which allowed me to become acquainted with Arnold Schwarzenegger and many other well known body builders and movie stars on the West coast. It also gave me the opportunity to land on the cover of *RoadKing* magazine and to have a career in health and fitness coaching. I was also able to see every single one of these United States except Hawaii and Alaska. Don't get me wrong, trucking can be hard, grueling work but it has its perks. Someone asked me recently why all of my knuckles were so dark. They have been that way for over 34 years from bruising them while pulling those chains and cables tight to secure a load. I am still tying down loads now just in a different way. This is Life! Nevertheless, this keeps me humble.

While many things change, the most fundamental things remain the same. At some time, sooner or later, we all have to learn about Grace, Mercy and Hope. I offer this little book up to you for consideration and a partial roadmap on your over the road trip called Life.

Be blessed,
Maurice Blair

## Life's Seven Basic Mile Markers

My seventeenth year of life was a really big one for me. I graduated from high school and one year later got married and then had my first child! I had some really hard choices to make. Chief among them was figuring out how to take care of all of us...me, my wife and our baby. So, I went to work for my daddy driving over the road. For the next seventeen years my life was measured in mile markers. Yep, to this day, when I pull up a memory from the road, it is in a file box in my mind labeled something like 'Mile Marker 175 just outside of Albuquerque' or 'Mile Marker 208, approaching the Canadian border'. Most mile markers carry memories of happy times. Some mile markers are not even slightly happy. But what they all have in common are lessons and blessings. A chance to see Hope and Faith fulfilled.

During my career as an over the road truck driver, I have come up with these seven mile markers of life. Some people may call them seven lessons and blessings of life. It's the same thing, but I choose to label them as "Life's Seven Basic Mile Markers". I started the numbers at Life Mile Marker 118. I read somewhere that by the time a child reaches six or seven years old the foundations of his character have been pretty much set by parental and environmental influences. So I just took the liberty of giving myself a 101 mile head start!

These Mile Markers are not locations, but represent significant milestones and lessons in my life.

## Life Mile Marker 118: Greatness

For my first mile marker, the lesson and the blessing is an understanding of **Greatness**. Driving on the road was humbling, very educational, very demanding and very rewarding. However, meeting the thousands and thousands of people that I was able to meet over my seventeen year career, I have to say they inspired me to be all that I can be and are a part of who I am today. I think it's amazing that sometimes we look for greatness in things and the mystique of people in high places. But depending on all kinds of people as I traveled, my amazing discovery was that greatness is laced through all of us.

Even though I drove a truck and saw places I never dreamed of, through the years I didn't feel totally satisfied. Fulfillment just wasn't there in the scenery or the sights. Mostly, at first, I spent a lot of time pouting because I thought my life was over before it started. I had to learn another way of seeing things to survive being so far out of my comfort zone. After all, I was just a young man trying to find my way.

What eventually gave me fulfillment was being able to meet people, speak with people, help inspire and motivate people to set short and long term goals. Sometimes it was no more than putting a smile on someone's face that fulfilled me. At other times it was the privilege of listening to a stranger's story and help them to come to grips with their own challenges. In the end, together, we learned a little more about all the ways that greatness can show up in each of us. Most of all, together we were blessed to determine our own definitions of greatness.

It opened my eyes to be able to travel the country, see people who were standing in need, and see people who were doing well. That actually struck a fire in me to get up and do better, because I saw on numerous occasions, that when you think you got it bad, I promise someone else has it worse. So, to complain, to chase after things that are fictitious and not real, it only sets us up for disappointment. To feel good, to feel worthy, to feel fulfilled, to be great, it all comes from being able to serve and be of assistance to others. That is **Greatness**!

## Life Mile Marker 128: Words

Yes, words are powerful. Riding miles and miles in a truck looking down on people gave me lots of time to examine the words that I was using to judge myself and what I was seeing. In fact, all this brain chatter caused me to develop a habit of seeking out libraries and book stores all around the country just so I could develop a better understanding of word choices and meanings. So, my second Life Mile Marker is **Words**.

I have to reflect back to when I was in the ninth grade. I was told by my math teacher in front of the entire class, "Blair, you ought to just go on ahead and quit school, drop out, because you are not going to amount to anything. You are not going to be anything." He said those words because it was challenging for me to catch on to where we were in the classroom with this particular section of math we were studying. He equated my inability to catch on, in a quick, timely fashion, to how the rest of my life was going to be. Those words not only hurt me, but they stuck with me and they stayed with me. They affected me for years and years to come, because he said them with the blatant intention to hurt. I never will forget that.

We have to be careful, because words are powerful. It took years of riding in that truck for me to understand and overcome that ninth grade blow to my self-measure. It is true that guns can kill. But before that, arguments, misunderstandings from the way we communicate, things we say, things we do, and how we respond to things with words make situations turn out badly or very ugly. That's what kills the spirit of a young lady or young man who could aspire to greatness. I never will forget that.

On the flip side of the same coin, I never will forget when I was driving; I delivered a load to Alberta, Canada. I was on my way back through Canada and had truck trouble. I had broken down; my transmission stopped working and I was unable to shift the fifteen gears. That breakdown caused my truck to be in the shop for about two and a half days. Therefore, I was not able to get home to spend Thanksgiving with my family. I was sad, frustrated and lonely.

I ran into a gentleman in Canada and he told me "Maurice, nothing is going to stay the same. These are things that happen in life." He actually sat me down and talked to me, a stranger, for about thirty minutes. The words he shared with me encouraged me and gave me great inspiration when I was in despair. Not only during that particular situation and moment, but also, even up to this point in time. It really moved me. It really affected me and showed me that words—yes, words—are powerful. You can use words or you can misuse words.

For this second mile marker in life, I encourage everyone to choose your **Word**s carefully. Choose how you use them. They can not only affect you, but can have a definite effect on others.

## Life Mile Marker 138: Love

My third mile marker in life is **Love**. Now that's a very broad and deep subject. It's very, very heavy. When I was traveling the highways and byways, I would see some of the simplest acts of love. Sometimes they were words spoken on a seemingly small level like "good morning, how are you doing, how is your day going." These, to a person in need, are momentary configurations of concern, even love.

On the other side of that coin, I saw some of the bigger gestures that were ugly; constructed as road rage; being inconsiderate or rude to a waitress, when she was trying to do the best job she could do during that time or moment. A simple act of asking for directions could turn into the ugliness of being made to think you are a bother, an intrusion or just plain stupid for not knowing.

Going back to the top side of that coin I have to honestly say, for me, traveling the highways and byways was love on its greatest level. Even on the smallest and simplistic of levels, the ability to recognize, give and receive love learned on the road, continues to sustain and encourage me today. As a man fully grown and still growing, I know that love is the most powerful force on this earth. What would make me say that is concern and love from relatives, friends, parents and even strangers who just stopped what they were doing and took their time to give me guidance, by showing me the way and encouraging me throughout this journey. Like I said, that helps sustain me even in this present time as a man.

The world is about love. You have a lot of bad things in this world. We all know that. There will always be a lot of bad things going on, but nothing supersedes and outshines the ability of a person to show concern, care and love toward a fellow person to simply uplift the person.

Yep, **Love** is the most powerful force on this planet.

## Life Mile Marker 148: The Process

**The Process** is the fourth mile marker in life. For everything we know and do there is a process, whether it's starting a garden, or raising a child to grow into a successful young lady or man. It even includes moving up because of a promotion on a job, raising your level of education or even developing yourself as an adult to become a better person and role model. Truly, everything is a process and it's unavoidable.

This was one of my most difficult mile markers on the road. Driving allowed me to better appreciate going through the process of life. I would leave Memphis, Tennessee with a load going to the next state over, or the east coast to Bangor, Maine, or Boston, Massachusetts, or wherever I would be delivering a load knowing each destination was an integrate part of the process. That whole trip was a series of processes that had to take place correctly and efficiently in order for me to be successful at my final destination. The same things apply when you are setting short and long term goals.

We live in a society where we want instant gratification. We want it right now at this moment, and we forget that the most important part in the getting is what we become in the process.

I would like to constantly encourage everyone to pay attention to the process. The process is what produces the outcome or the result which we are seeking. The process is unavoidable, but the process is more important than the outcome in certain cases, meaning it's about being able to prepare and adjust during the process. Like the old saying goes, 'everyone wants to be successful but very few want to prepare to be successful'. So again, I want to encourage my readers to never overlook the process. The details are in the process. Success is in **The Process**!

## Life Mile Marker 158: Suffering

My fifth mile marker in life is **Suffering**. That's something we are all going to become acquainted with directly or indirectly. As we live our lives, we are going to be exposed to some type of suffering. Be it mental suffering, physical suffering, emotional suffering, financial suffering; we all will become acquainted with it at some point in time in our lives. However, it's not permanent unless we choose for it to become permanent.

I read somewhere, "Pain is optional and suffering is a choice." There are many, many hurts that bring us pain. Yet, it is our perceptions and the choices we make about the pain that takes us in or out of suffering!

I remember times when I would have to leave my home and go on the road when the need to leave was painful. Whether it was my daughter's or son's birthday, my wife's birthday, or a specific function that was going on at my kids' school that I was not going to be able to attend, it would bring some disappointment to me. More importantly, when I would leave out on the road going to my destination to deliver my load, I couldn't really say I would be back in three days or a designated time. This is because once I delivered my load, there could be other situations and circumstances that would occur that might prohibit me from getting home at that particular time and day. Imagine the hurt of not even being able to give my word or commitment to make it back in addition to missing out on whatever important function, engagement or outing occurring.

I dealt with a lot of internal and emotional suffering that I had to transform into a passing hurt. How? I am here to tell you nothing lasts forever. I am here to tell you that you have the power to change your response from suffering to a passing hurt. We get to suffer, we just don't have to allow the suffering to last beyond the time needed to teach us the lesson and give us the blessing. The important thing is to do whatever is necessary and appropriate to express and release the suffering for ourselves and those around us.

I never will forget I was leaving San Francisco, CA, and got a phone call from my mother saying my grandmother was about to pass away, and she was calling my name wanting to speak with me. I was over 2,000 miles away from her. I was not able to get to her. That was one of the most emotional, toughest trips I have ever had to endure and was repeated with my wife's grandmother passing. I felt very helpless that I could not be there to console my wife in whatever way that I could. In both instances, I had to choose between simply using the time on the way back, to process my grief and be stronger when I finally arrived, or let my pain morph into guilt that I could use to beat myself up and suffer over forever.

Life is about enduring. We were created by the Creator to be able to endure pain and hardships. Sometimes we give up on ourselves too easily or too quickly for no rhyme or reason. Suffering is something we will all become acquainted with, but we all will be able to endure or overcome in time and that is what choice is all about. So, let's not allow our suffering to become final.

Even more so, let's not allow our suffering to become fatal, as we live on this earth. Let us not become walking zombies over past sufferings because someone's careless actions, past hurtful events or something we may not have been able to accomplish. Let's not carry that around with us. Let's not allow that to walk in us as we walk around doing our day to day tasks, year after year, becoming walking zombies in a perpetual personal pity party.

## Life Mile Marker 168: Longevity

My sixth mile marker in life is **Longevity**. I found that during my 17 years of driving, it was easy to become a pretty good driver the first six months, first year, the second year, the third year, the fourth year. But true success is about longevity.

Can you still maintain a certain level of excellence year after year after year in whatever endeavor you choose? Longevity (and that goes for whether you are in school or a career), requires sustainability. Can you sustain your will, your curiosity and use a positive work ethic to maintain your GPA or that level of excellence that takes you higher and higher in achievement? Can you demonstrate longevity or staying power as a good student that leads you to being a good and desirable employee? That's what it's about—longevity. It was not so much about how or why I started the job, but I had to ask myself if I wanted to be successful in trucking.

I met a lot of people who were happy and many who were not happy in trucking. I knew it took that sustainability factor to be able to carry out and deliver at a high level as a truck driver. It just wasn't about delivering my load from point A to point B, it was about coming into contact with people. It was about being able to work well with shippers, customers and the people I met along the way in various restaurants, fuel stops, job sites and various other places. We all have our good days and bad days. Life is not a straight line. It's full of ups and downs. Even during that time, it's about being able to stick and stay. Anyone can be great; anybody can do well for a short period of time. But, can we do the things necessary to operate on a high level consistently through our tenure of that particular life which we are a part of? Being able to do that through trucking really helped me tremendously.

Toward the end of my trucking career, I could see some of my abilities diminishing, but that comes with everything you do. You are not going to be as sharp at 41 as you are at 21. That's just a part of life, but it's still about the quality of what you do and not necessarily the quantity. It also has to do with paying attention to diminishing skill and recognizing when it means that it's time to do something new.

Quantity and quality matter. It is essential to be able to go that full entire mile marker and making it to the next one while sustaining yourself in greatness. It's very important, that whatever you set out to do in life to count the cost, measure the distance and commit to performing at high levels year after year after year, until life gives you a new, better route with a new set of lessons and blessings.

## Life Mile Marker 178: Reality

**Reality**. This is my seventh and last mile marker in the basic list. Reality is what it is. It's reality.

Several times I came face to face with reality during my time traveling up and down the highways and byways. There were a couple times when I was involved in an accident. One particular accident almost took my life in El Paso, TX. That was a big strong dose of reality for me. Another time was when I was able to be featured on the cover of a nationwide magazine in 1998. I was also featured on that same magazine cover in the summer of 2015. Being featured on the cover twice (I am the only person to have done that) of *RoadKing Magazine* that was a big dose of reality hitting me in my face.

The first level of reality when I was involved in that accident in El Paso showed me that at any moment your life can be taken. We never know what tomorrow brings. As a matter of fact, we never know what the end of the day brings. However, that reality constantly remind us that we should live in the moment and be thankful in the moment. Sometimes we spend so much time wishing and looking forward to something we desire in the far away future until we do not enjoy or take advantage of what's around us in the moment. My realities taught me that.

My second big dose of reality was the great truth that anything is possible. I was a mere 36 years old when I was first featured on the cover of *RoadKing Magazine*. Seventeen years later, there I was again. It happened because I had the nerve to believe if I called them with the idea, all they could do was say yes or no. And they said yes!

It makes me reflect on the name of this book, *From No Where to Now Here,* meaning that we may not understand it, we may not even see it. But the reality is that opportunity is always in us and around us, whether we take advantage of it right during that moment in time, or we have to get up and go create it in that moment. Opportunity is always present. So, be appreciative of each moment. Let's not set our sights so far ahead that we neglect the things that are going on in our lives within that moment, within that hour, within that day. Don't forgo today's opportunity looking for something that is to come.

A lot of times, if we are honest with ourselves, we set ourselves up for disappointment when we look too far ahead. Setting goals can be a tricky thing. The trick is remembering that what we do in the present moment creates the next moment, and the past cannot be undone or redone. Once you achieve a goal; stop, take a deep breath, congratulate yourself and savor the moment before rushing off to the next goal.

Sitting in a truck cab, all alone, pulling a wide load gives a person a lot of time to dream, plan and wish. We can take that time to judge ourselves and come up short, or use it to become a better human being. I was blessed to journey from No Where to Now Here. The work that I was doing, moving goods all over the country taught me the value of being here, now. It's all we've got and it's enough when we use these seven mile markers and all the others we pick up on the journey.

## More Mile Markers For Life

I want to expand more on the Mile Markers based on what may be called expanded takeaways or *Mile Markers for Life.* These words are for men, women, children—anyone who aspires to be successful in the midst of unplanned road trips. In spite of how it may seem, every trip defines a place where we learn to better lead in our own lives so that we might earn the right to lead others. No matter how you look at it, potential just never runs out.

I would like to begin by saying I have been inspired to write this book because of the vision of those who have sacrificed and suffered to make this life better for us. The highest form of appreciation that we can show them is by always doing and being the best that we can be. Because we are the hope of their dreams, I feel we, as a people and as a society, have not lived up to our potential. Somewhere along the path we have failed those who came before us and have lost our way.

There is something I want you to always keep in mind. Make this paramount. Make this first. I want you to understand that physical, emotional and intellectual conditioning can mean success or failure for any person who is trying to accomplish certain goals or get through challenging times in their lives. Just like we condition our bodies—we may lift weights, run, jog or some other exercise—but even more so important than all of that, is the conditioning of the mind and controlling your emotions.

The conditioning of your mind and controlling your emotions...Yes, that is and will determine success or failure in whatever goal you are trying to accomplish. When the controversial storms of life beat us down; soak us to the bone with heartache, disappointment and setbacks, we must always harbor the hope and the faith that circumstances are ever changing. That which seemed so awful may turn out to be the best thing to ever happen to you.

Tying this all in with what I have just said, we must understand that our lives have a birth date and an expiration date. It's no different than milk, bread, eggs and other things that can perish! What sets us apart is that in between those two dates we have a choice to live a meaningless life or a meaningful life. Yes, there are going to be some things that will happen in our lives that will cause us to choose one or the other. However, you will see the people who make it in this life—the people who are successful—make sacrifices. They don't do the things the way everyone else does them. They break away from the crowd and perform those tasks necessary to become successful and make it through this life. Regardless of the situation, they never lower their standards to fit the common, over used mold. By following their example, you automatically become the beneficiary of the good things that life has to offer.

Yes, it's true that in life trials and tribulations will come, but our decisions and reactions under pressure often make us responsible for our own failures and successes during that time. Also, I urgently need you to remember it's your character and your courage, along with your talent—*and* the faith in yourself—that will carry you beyond life's setbacks and failures. We all overlook these components from time to time. We must keep them in sight to maneuver beyond the obstacles.

In today's time, so many of us are giving up. So many of us are turning to drugs and alcohol as a solution for life's let downs. So many of us are unwilling to discipline ourselves, in order to handle the pressures of day-to-day living, whether it's pressure stemming from a job, school, peers, etc. Despite the storm clouds of controversy raining on our physical, emotional or intellectual pursuits, we must persevere. It's easy to take what seems like the carefree open road that everyone is traveling, but always be mindful of the road less chosen. Given time that road will bring us to our desired destination.

Yes, it's true that we want to succeed, but we must understand we have to prepare ourselves for success. We all want to score big in this game. We all want to pass this particular test, this exam or obtain this degree. We want, we want, we want. But too often we do not want to prepare ourselves for the difficult tasks that lie ahead. These tough times, these great experiences we go through, generate character and character produces great people.

During these times in your life, during life's trials and tribulations, you must be able to produce a precise résumé of patience, perseverance, as well as smart work and hard work. As you work your way through life, no one has the power to hold you back, if you, as an individual, become a thinker. Now, what do I mean by that? Become a critical thinker, an analytical thinker and most of all a positive thinker. As you embrace these three levels of thinking you have to continue to work with great energy day after day after day.

Within the work and the personal sacrifice, only time alone will stand between you and what you are trying and wanting to accomplish. During these hardships and disappointments, don't break your concentration. Just continue to work through it. If you do that, if you work through it and embrace self-sacrifice your chances of reaching your goal are magnified. You will reach your goal.

Many of us tend to think of self-sacrifice as negative; having to give up all pleasure and living a life of boredom. Actually, research has shown that to move from one situation to a greater and more fulfilling one, we often have to give up some relationships, people, beliefs and ideas that may be holding us back. Maybe the sacrifice is temporary, but it is nearly always necessary. Please understand, self-sacrifice is the real miracle out of which all miracles grow which ushers in divine intervention, not design intervention. It allows us to be able to knock down the obstacles, the mountains that are in our lives, one stone at a time.

There is no time like the present to start living your life with assurance; with goals; with purpose; with intention. Don't become laminated in laziness or paralyzed by fear. You have to be willing to risk the occasional failures for future success. Look within yourself. Find out what drives you. What are the particular things that drive you day in and day out to want to achieve or continuously improve your life and get better as a person? What are those things that allow you to obtain the certain successes necessary in your life? What are your strengths? Know your weakness and find a way to strengthen them!

Personally, I am driven by my own, as well as family misfortunes that have risen up over the years. I want to be more, do more, have more and see more. Not because they were less, but because they dreamed and never got there. Life is a test of will more than anything else. It's a marathon not a sprint. The long haul demands patience and rewards those who persevere.

For example, I remember breaking down on the road in the bitter cold and having to walk and try to hitch hike to the next town that was ten miles away. The reality in that time, for me, was that drivers on the road would rarely pick up African-American strangers. This became for me a severe test of will power over skill power. If I wanted to get that truck off the road, I had to persevere.

Your discipline, your work ethic and your ability to serve others will be a testament of your greatness. Yes, you have to believe you can create a life that will differentiate your life from one of mediocrity. You have to drive out complacency by pushing yourself harder and harder and smarter and smarter. When you allow excellence to become habitual, there is no end to your greatness.

Now don't misunderstand me, when you fail or when you lose, that does not by any means imply that you are not great. The greatest people that have ever lived have failed numerous times at one thing—or many things. When you fail or when you lose, make sure it is never because of a lack of your best efforts!

From the beginning, too often we allow our starting point to become our finish line. It's about having confidence in self and having confidence in life. You build confidence through many types of experiences and that doesn't come easy. In all your doing, don't mistake activity for accomplishments. Just because you are out here trying to do this or trying to do that, does not mean that you are working towards accomplishing your goal. That's what I mean by not mistaking activity for accomplishments. You can be involved actively doing this or occupied with that, but are you actually accomplishing your goals? Is it actually getting you where you want to go? Is it actually getting you from point A to point B? In fact, do you even know where you want to go? You can just be going through the motions. It's not what you do; it's how you do what you do. Also, you have to have that mindset to maintain the momentum to carry you from start to finish; from one goal to the next goal to the next goal and so on.

It won't be easy. It's difficult to maintain a consistent level of excellence. You have to be willing to meet every challenge, to cross every bridge, to travel through the furnace of affliction in order to come out of the other side successful. In the midst of seeking to accomplish these things; in the midst of trying to become successful in your own endeavors, ask yourself these two questions:

- Do I live to express or do I live to impress?
- Do I work for applause or do I work for a cause?

Understand that everything we seek to do or set out to do, should have relevance to it. It should have substance to it. It should have meaning and purpose. I don't think we achieve lasting success unless we add another ingredient to that mixture. That ingredient is to serve a cause greater than self. That is what lasting success is all about. Personal gain is empty if you do not feel you have positively touched another's life.

We are not obligated to be wealthy or an athlete, entertainer or even a doctor or lawyer to be considered successful. We are only obligated to do and to give our best and to be a productive member of society, not a destructive one. You alone set the standard for what it means to succeed in life.

It is you alone who knows what will truly fulfill you in your heart and make your life worth living. Please understand, none of us knows what tomorrow will bring. Still, the best way to somewhat predict the future is to create it. You create your future by the way you approach everything that happens to you <u>today</u>—be it good or bad. May I add, there are no "secrets" to success, so don't waste your time looking for them.

## Greatness

Somewhere during our act of moving forward, we lost the true meaning and essence of who we really are. Somewhere we lost our grip on what was supposed to be greatness. Most of us have forgotten the true meaning of greatness and self-worth. Instead of pursuing that which should have pushed us forward into a positive direction, we got caught up in the trap of failure; often viewing greatness as some impossible dream.

For me, true greatness is not what I do, but rather what I inspire in others to do, which overall would enhance the quality of their lives. So, is not the whole purpose of life to live a life of purpose? For me, success without fulfillment of my purpose is nothing but failure.

What is your definition of greatness? We know all too well the definition of failure. We experience it time and time again. We may feel it in a failed exam or in an unsuccessful project at work. We feel the effects of its harsh disappointment in losing at a game we thought we should have won. Or maybe it's the loss of a loved one through a disastrous, incompetent relationship.

All of those things can be heartbreaking. However, losing your self-worth and your will to thrive is the greatest tragedy of all. Once you become *un*acquainted with who you are, it's easy for your life to start sliding down the slippery slope to disaster. When we fail, we may lose sight of what's really important.

I have learned that the two most important days of our lives are:
    (1) The day we are born; and
    (2) The day we realize why we were born.

These two intangibles play a very important role in self-worth. We must never forget that we are a product of privilege and prepared for a purpose. The privilege is all of the sacrifices made on our behalf in the past!

We must constantly remind ourselves of our purpose in life. I cannot believe that the sole purpose of this life is to just be happy. I believe that the purpose of life is to be useful; to be responsible; to be compassionate; to count for something other than ourselves. We should make some impact; some difference, in order to show that we have lived at all.

This brings us back full circle to self-worth. Too often we embrace the concept of learned helplessness. This learned helplessness shows up as accepting defeat, or that it is okay to be trapped in a life of mediocrity. All too often, this concept has become imbedded in our homes, our schools, and even as present day practitioners of our own vocations.

So again, I would like to ask you: *What is your definition of greatness?* Are you willing to go outside your comfort zone to achieve it?

## Words

*"Sticks and stones may break my bones, but words can never hurt me."*

Don't believe it. Don't believe it for one second. Don't ever underestimate the power of words. Words properly used can help mend a broken heart or inspire and give hope to a homeless individual. They can also bring two hearts together rewarding them with a lifetime of love. They can also inspire an individual with a terminal illness to fight through another day. But misused, words can cause heartache and pain. Awkward and mishandled words can cause countries to rival against each other; families, friends, co-workers, and even neighbors to fall apart. Words that trigger hate and disloyalty can even result in death.

I want you to stop. Take a minute, look back and reflect on the impact of how words have helped you or have harmed you. How words have inspired others to be all that they can be and be the best that they actually can be. How words have made or changed the face of our nation. Now take a moment and look at how negative words can spark a reaction that can kill a dream or result in the loss of life.

Stop and take a look around. Take a look at how negative words have created anger that has distorted some of our homes, our workplaces, our communities, and yes, even our country. Look at how the power of words has caused us to drift into darkness. Look at how the power of words has caused us to become unacquainted with who we really are and why we were really created. We weren't created to beef, to bully, to destroy or to hate one another. We must not allow the chains of arrogance, ignorance and hatred to confine us or define us. We have lost the love and luster of respect for one another. Look at how the lack of respect is driving us, as a community, as a society; as a country. We have become the connoisseurs of hatred and disrespect.

Don't get me wrong. We have always had issues. As long as there has been a world, there have always been issues. But years ago, we used to pride ourselves on respect. We took pride in being respectful. "Yes ma'am, yes sir; no ma'am, no sir, excuse me; how may I help you". Sometimes we hear those words from the past echoed, but not often. I have to stop and ask myself: is being respectful dead?

Now let's ask ourselves how can we counteract that? How can we untie this knot that we have tied? Well, in order to activate real change, we must start with that man or that woman in the mirror. We must start with ourselves. As the old saying goes, we change the man *then* we change the world. We must first start with ourselves or there will be no change at all.

As a motivational coach, I 100% understand that we can't change people. People have to change and want change for themselves. My job is to help inspire you to make a change because I can't change you. My work is to remind you and to have faith in your God-given ability for greatness. We all can be inspired to do better, to live better, and to perform better. Whether it's in our homes, whether it's on a team we are involved with, in sports, in our classroom or churches. When it comes down to it, change is up to us as individuals first, before we can come together collectively to create real change.

It is with certainty, there are going to be times when we are going to be misunderstood when doing our acts of kindness. However, we must remain faithful and diligent because it's not about seeking applause or praise in what we do. It's about making the next person better and making ourselves better in the process. We are not seeking stardom or sacrificing individual achievement. That's not what it's about. That is not what *we* are about. It's about creating something new; creating something better by becoming better people.

## Love

I must say I don't feel that there's a problem on this earth that cannot be solved or at least made better through love. Love is one of the most used words, and misused words of all time. It is one of those words that we throw around with little or no meaning to it.

In relationships, we may express love through the acronym: L-O-V-E (**Lusting Over Various Emotions**). But that is not what real love is. Real love is having the ability to stick it out; to stick and stay; to work things out. It means being able to flex and compromise without breaking. Love is long suffering. Love is encouragement. Love is standing in the midst of heated battles and not being interested in having the last word. Love is being flexible, able to accommodate. Love is being understanding. Love is being firm but fair. You must give love in order to get love. You don't always get in life what you want. You get in life what you are. It's not about where we are; it's about who we are. We have to be willing to die to who we have been, in order to give birth to who we can become. Our love should be a continuous progression; an emotional engagement of unshakable optimism.

Yes, of course through love we can suffer pain. We can hang tight to hope in a hopeless situation. We can nurture unrealistic expectations. We are plagued occasionally by our fears, hurts and the heartbreak that love can bring. However, is it not love that has brought us this far? Back in the day there was a song that asked: "What's love got to do with it?" However, when we learn how to love ourselves and others, Love has everything to do with it.

There must always be a continuing goal to make increasing our knowledge of the importance of giving love; of sharing love; and actively participating in bearing the fruit of love. As Booker T. Washington would say, "cast down your bucket where you are". That could mean several things, but to me that means right where you are, right where you stand in life, be all that you can be. Give all that you can give. Help those who are standing in need and want to be helped. Everything is accomplished through love. This world was created because of a love often beyond our comprehension.

True love can untie that knot of hatred, anger, bigotry, jealously, and destruction. True love can bring these so-called gangs together. True love can mend broken hearts. True love can also give hope to the hopeless. No, there is no more powerful force on this earth than love.

Facing the storms of life begins with knowing that they will come. But, how we face the storms is very important. Life is the ultimate test of love, dedication and will. Through love, we can be strong and take one more step towards the top of the hill of life, no matter how weary we may be. Love will cause us to run into a burning building! I can't emphasize it enough, but true love comes with a responsibility. The world can be a dangerous place, not because of those that do evil but because of those who look on and do nothing.

This concept brings me to the point most people need to learn in life: how to "love people and use things" instead of "using people and loving things". So many people have gone out on a limb looking for love. So many people have sacrificed their personal lives and safety in search of love. Love does require us to take stands; to take risks. It also requires us to take responsibility.

Is it not love to watch a mother run back into a burning house to save her child? Is that not love to watch a parent or your parents sacrifice by working day and night so that you can have a better life than they have? Is that not love for parents to want for their child to have the best opportunity, the best education, to have a leg up in life that will give them an opportunity to be successful?

All of those are risks. When you speak of that, everything is a risk, but it is all out of love. And, at the same time it's laced with a responsibility. Love is being responsive. Love is unyielding. We can say that we love what we do but with love comes responsibility. I tell people all the time that when we set out every day in life, of course we are taking a chance and a risk, but it is all out of love. We may or may not love what we do. It's the reward afterwards that really counts; that moves us, that pushes us, that keeps us soldiering on which confirms that one does not fall in love or out of love. One grows in love. The process at times is more important than the results.

Yes, we are seeking the results. That's the magnet that pulls us there. However, the process itself—good times and bad times—are those things that allow us to create memories. Those are the things that strengthen us and reinforce who we are. The love that we have inside strengthens us. Those are the things that are most important—that really shapes us as individuals. Therefore, we may not be in love with what we do or whatever, but we can grow to learn and grow into that type of love because of the reason behind it.

The only thing that we can never get enough of is love. The only thing that we can never give enough of is love. If one wishes to know love, one must live love. Love is an action verb. However, love does not always begin and end the way we seem to think it should. Love can be a battle. Sometimes love can be war. Love is just growing up; experiencing those things I call unavoidable sufferings. We look forward to the time when the power of love will replace the love of power. Then will our communities, our families, our schools, our churches, the world in general know the blessings of peace.

    Throughout the years, whenever darkness or gloom has touched my life, it has been my strong unmovable faith and a great network of friends that have carried me through the troubled waters and given me the strength to carry on. I know that love is at the center of that equation. I have to honestly say, it was through love that I have been able to keep moving forward even in troubling and challenging times. The thing I like about love is that we can only learn to love by loving. However, the greatest weakness of most humans is their hesitancy to tell others how much they love them while they are still alive.

    So ask yourself: What's your definition of love? What does love mean to you? How can you take love and go out and spread it and make your world a better world? Who do you need to tell right now that you love them and the wonderful reasons why?

## The Process

For many of us, our lives—whether we want to admit it or not—are like forests; wild and all over the place. There is no structure; and that is why we never accomplish what we set out to achieve—and why we don't have the things we really want in life.

You should be positive and think positive. Set goals and make every effort to reach them. Your life should be very intentional; very deliberate. Be very intentional with the time you wake up in the morning; and the time you go to bed. Be very intentional. Be very deliberate about what you eat. Be very deliberate about your education. Be very deliberate about the people you bring into your life, the books you read and the things you watch on television. Your mind set and the things you do from day to day should shape you into the person you want to be—not the person you accidentally become.

Now let me be very clear on something. Positive thinking will get you nowhere, if you are not willing to get up and put some hustle behind your muscle. In other words, every dream, every level of accomplishment and every level of success begins with a thought. That thought is a preview of coming attractions which is all about delayed gratification. Delayed gratification is not negative. It is all about getting something in the future by putting in the work first.

It's kind of like comparing a forest to a garden. You may want to ask yourself this question: Is my life like a forest or a garden? Both are beautiful and both are very much needed. The forest is wild and uncontrolled; you know, stuff is all over the place. However, the garden is the result of someone who has done something very intentional; very deliberate. They've lined everything up just so. They've chosen specific plants and placed them strategically for maximum effect. Moreover, they have purposefully tended the garden, not missing a need or removing invasive, unwelcomed growth.

I remember back in March of 2012, I needed to have a hip replacement. It was something that I couldn't get around; something that I had to do because I was having excruciating pain in my left hip. During that same year I was turning fifty; a time when some people, especially men, go through a mid-life crisis. Most guys want to jump up and buy exotic cars, dress differently, do anything to deny the aging process! But those particular things didn't tempt me. I am a man who loves to dress nice, look good, and to be neat, so *this* played into my need to have the surgery, and to recover as soon as possible. I wanted to maintain my own personal style that I so loved and my hip was cramping my style! That meant I needed to set a goal.

So, I had the hip replacement in March and in August I would turn 50. I wanted to be completely healed by then, and maybe even do better than before. So I challenged myself. I hadn't competed in a body building competition in like 17 years. So I said, "You know what, after this hip replacement, I'm going to compete again." So, I made the decision to compete. I didn't just want to compete locally, I wanted to go away to really test and challenge myself, so I chose a competition in Kansas.

After my hip replacement, I rehabbed and went through physical therapy. Then after physical therapy, I had about three months of rigorous training, twice a day, six days a week, with no days off, to ready myself for the body building competition that September. (In body-building the seventh day is a rest day.) It was an undertaking and experience that I had, to become reacquainted with from my younger years.

I had a lot of naysayers to tell me, "Maurice, you won't do well." Or someone would ask, "Why are you trying to do this? What does it prove?" Well, the purpose was not necessarily to win, but to meet the challenge head on and accomplish the goal. I didn't know if I would place first or place last. It was the process that was important. The process is what counts. I tell people all the time, goals are important but it's not what you achieve in that particular goal, that's not it. You don't put a period behind that. It's what you become *during* the process of obtaining that goal that counts. It was like I was a new Maurice. I had to challenge myself like never before; push myself like never before.

So the time came for me to compete and I went out to Kansas. It was a whole new ballgame from what I was familiar with in the past, but I ended up placing 1$^{st}$ in my age group. I had turned 50, of course, but I won first place in the 50 year-old division! I won first place in my weight class. I look back and say, "That's what it's about." You have to fall in the love with the process of accomplishment! We all have dreams. Some want to be rich. Some want to play in the NFL. Others may want to be a doctor, a lawyer, etc. All of that is cool. However, the process is what's important.

I feel most people want to jump over the work or the process and get straight to the goal. They don't want to have to embrace that delayed gratification. I've learned that the process works in any facet of life, whether you're trying to obtain a college degree, be it here or abroad; or if you want to be a successful artist. It doesn't matter what the goal is. You have to fall in love with the process. Once you do that, it makes the journey a little bit sweeter. That is what will really build you; mold you—the process. Each step is an opportunity to build and to improve; to carry out the tasks in order to reach your ultimate accomplishment.

But remember. You don't obtain that accomplishment overnight. You set out to obtain it over time by putting in work; putting in hours every single day on every activity and every task that is going to help you become the person you dreamed of becoming when you first began. Also, take advantage of the opportunities along the way. There are opportunities everywhere, in every walk of life, in every area of human endeavor, to achieve human success. You have to seize the opportunities and make the most of them.

## Suffering

The next phase in this journey of self-enrichment is suffering. One measure of a person's greatness is their capacity for suffering. Nothing good comes cheaply. Let me say that again. Nothing good comes cheaply.

Sometimes we have to go through things; to suffer through things, so we shouldn't be surprised when we meet the hard while going for the best. Hard times are not quit times. You see, in our daily trials, we will either choose to give up or give in or give it all we've got. Suffer through the tough times. Don't give up. If you do, you will train yourself to give up every time you face difficulties. You might miss the realization that through struggle, through suffering, some of the best lessons become stepping stones to improvement.

There is suffering in life and there are defeats. No one can avoid them. It is better to lose some of the battles in the struggle for your dreams, than to be defeated without ever knowing what you are actually fighting for. That goes back to your purpose.

It has been said that in today's society, we have lesser minds but bigger wallets; bigger houses and less wealth; more food but declining health; more friends but less love. We have bigger schools but less learning; more books, but less reading. All of this leads to suffering when we thought things were getting better. It is this view that causes many of us who seek happiness and joy to feel so discouraged.

Struggle and suffering are in the world, but does it really have to be? We have to be diligent and wise about what we want. We have to apply ourselves to achieve what we want. Sometimes we may need to differentiate between needs and wants. Narcissism and immediate gratification can dim our vision and trip us up. Our goals need purpose supported by intelligent and purposeful struggle.

The key is to rebuild your thinking. Develop the self-discipline to take complete control of your mental attitude. Permanent results only come from permanent change and lifestyle. Why should the way I feel depend on the thoughts in someone else's world? The world cares very little about what a man or woman knows. It's what a person is able to do that counts. The pain and suffering of sorrow can strengthen the mind and make us break down barriers, overcome and set new limits. After all of the suffering and hardships, through all of that, the secret to getting ahead in this world is first getting started. Also a secret is to not get addicted to the suffering and struggle, but to simply use it as points of reference.

You can't let laziness or fear get in the way of your dreams. Each of us has a born gift or talent that makes certain things easy for us. This is why all things are not a struggle for all people. The thing that comes easy for you is your gift and it is to be used to grow your weaknesses. Too often we fail to acknowledge our gifts simply because they do come easy.

Ask yourself this question: How hungry are you to improve? How big is your appetite for success? You must develop the mindset to say I will conquer what has never been conquered. I will train my mind and my body will follow. I will move further and fight harder than any of my opponents.

We must understand that no one is alone in their troubles. There is always someone else thinking, rejoicing, or suffering in the same way that gives us strength to confront the challenges before us. Does that include suffering for love? Yes, that includes everything. For there is suffering and it is best to accept it because it won't go away because you pretend it is not there. Then again, you have to know when and how to let it go. Stop turning on your emotional television to watch the same program over and over again. The show that reminds you of how much you suffered from a certain loss is only poisoning you and you alone. Stop complaining about your circumstances; get busy creating new ones. You either suffer the pain of discipline or the pain of regret. You get to choose. You have to understand that hard times are sometimes blessings in disguise. We may well have to suffer, but in the end we need to make sure it makes us stronger, better, and much wiser.

It is said that he who learns must suffer. Even in our sleep, pain that we cannot forget falls drop by drop upon our hearts robbing us of restful sleep. In our own despair, against our own will sometimes wisdom comes. Everyone suffers at least one bad betrayal in their lifetime. It's what unites us as humanity. The trick is not to let it destroy your trust in others when that happens. Don't let them take the joy of life from you.

The professionals, the successful ones, they are the ones who are willing to knock on the door of complete exhaustion every single day. The adversity you faced throughout your life has prepared you for this moment in time. If we examine the biographies of those historical figures that we recognize as being great, all earned their greatness by what they gave back to the world in music, philosophy, literature, commerce, medicine, and on and on. Success is a byproduct of giving back. It comes to those who are concentrating on something important beyond themselves. To succeed or even to survive these days demands an unending attention to detail.

Complacency can sabotage your job, your health and your family. It is and can be instructive to learn from the past and inspiring to build for the future. But the fact is both the road behind and the road ahead is nonexistent. We only have NOW.

I really wish that most people would understand that security never comes from contracts or employment arrangements; it comes from ability, skill and dedication. Any security has to come from within. It's something we have to carry around in our own heads. Sometimes even the briefest lapse in attention can create tragedy. One careless act can destroy a future.

Somewhere between the Industrial Revolution and the Information Age, it seems we have lowered our standards and our aim. We have compromised quality in the name of efficiency. For growing numbers of us, average has become an acceptable goal. Being good enough is just good enough. In today's world, excellence can determine not only success but survival. The difference between good and best can be razor thin.

We usually can find something positive in every negative situation if we look for it. Not everyone can go to college, but everyone can be educated. Things turn out best for people who make the best of the way things turn out. If you want to improve your life and enjoy a higher rate of success in everything you do, then make it a habit to say "I will". Remember there is no such phrase as *try* power; it is *will* power! Sometimes, the best things come from the worst things that happen to us.

There is plenty of evidence that we can do just about anything we want to do in our spare time. That is, once we stop killing it (time). When success comes to us late in our lives, it only means that we were allowed more time to prepare for it. Theodor Geisel's first book was turned down twenty-eight times by publishers before Vanguard finally accepted it. After that Geisel went on to write forty-six other books including two you are sure to recognize: *The Cat in the Hat* and *Green Eggs and Ham*. We know Theodor Geisel by his pen name, Dr. Seuss. See, Geisel's greatest story was not the one that he wrote; it was the one that he lived. It was a story of determination and perseverance; a story of a writer who stuck with it just a little longer.

Our greatest underdeveloped natural resource is us. Every day, for each of us, there are opportunities to make life better. We have to be tuned into the possibilities of them. Everybody feels the pain of failure; only the wise are able to move from them and move on. Truly successful people are always reaching, stretching. We all have said "only if I had done this or did that. If I only could have seen the end result." The important question is not the important opportunities you missed yesterday, but rather what doors are opening in front of you right now.

You have to do more than work hard in life to succeed. You have to work smart. That means, first and foremost, you need a plan, a strategy, a design, a map. If you are to realize your potential in life, you need a plan. Great works can only be accomplished by those who are intoxicated with a passion for greatness. Yes, you can turn lemons into lemonade; weeds into gardens, and pennies into fortunes simply by making a choice to do so.

It's a funny thing how people doubt their beliefs but believe their doubts. I'm not saying we have to be perfect. Perfection is a goal that can never be reached. But, it must be your objective. Work unceasingly to improve. Remember, it's the quality of your effort that counts the most. Not your effort, but the quality of it. Yes, for all of us there should be joy in the journey, but we must also know it will bring its share of, suffering, strife, struggle and frustrations. How you deal with it determines how it deals with you.

You must be focused on your work, not your job. We leave one job, take another job, leave that job, and go to another job. Your work, along with your family, should be the linchpin for your existence. That's something that you can hang your hat on. Because living in this day and time requires that you have both character and conviction. Having character is much more important than being a character. Along with character I would like to add class. Class is a very hard thing to define. However, once you see it, you will never forget it.

During the process of tough and challenging times, never let your head hang down. Never give up, sit down and just grieve. Find a way. Don't pray when it rains if you don't pray when the sun shines. Good things happen to those who hustle. Even in the most impossible situations, stand tall and keep your head up, shoulders back; keep moving, running, looking up; demonstrating your pride, dignity and defiance. You may have to double your efforts because complacency is prohibited.

## Longevity

A component that goes hand in hand with suffering is longevity.

The dictionary's definition of longevity is a long individual life or great duration of an individual life. It is also recognized as a length of service or tenure. In reference to longevity, it's about having the sustainability and the stick-to-it-ness to stay the course--to stay on chart. I've discovered that in order to be successful at whatever endeavor you choose, it's going to require that an individual has longevity. Any of us can do well for a short span or period of time. However, to really be successful, where it has a lasting effect, it must be laced with longevity.

Let's take a look at a child or an adult who chooses to enroll in school. It is not enough to just begin; continuance is necessary. Mere enrollment will not make you a scholar. The student must continue in school through the long course until he or she masters each class or grade level. Success depends upon your staying power. The reason for failure in most cases is the lack of persistence. Lack of staying the course and finishing the course--that's a part of longevity.

The education you receive is a social process. Education is growth. Education is not preparation for life. In actuality, education is life itself. Perseverance is that link or that chain link to longevity. Nothing is given away. What you get, you earn with diligence and intelligence.

Imagine the reward you receive after working on something long after others have given up; it's amazing! You see, a champion or a successful person does not give up. He or she *gets up* when adversity hits. The donkey stays down; the thoroughbred responds to pressure in a positive way. Life is like a grindstone. Whether it grinds you down or polishes you up, depends on you. It depends on what you are made of.

Adversity is the reality of life. You are never really sure when it's going to come or how long it's going to stay. But the way you handle it is a direct reflection of your character as a person. The person who graduates today and stops learning tomorrow is uneducated the day after. Understand that it's a tireless effort, but that's how you succeed. You never quit. You keep on going day and night. No matter how much you think you've sacrificed or suffered, there are thousands of others who have done the same and given as much or more of themselves.

You see, giving up reinforces a sense of incompetence, but going on gives you a commitment to success. Real difficulties can be overcome. It's only the imaginary ones that are unconquerable. Falling into the deepest valley is nothing to fear. It just means that you are in the position to climb the world's highest mountain. I hear people talk about pressure. I listen to students who come and tell me "Mr. Blair, I'm under so much pressure to pass this exam." Well, pressure comes from being unprepared.

Undertake something that is difficult. Too many people are thinking of security instead of opportunity. They seem to be more afraid of life than they are of being afraid of death. In other words, don't allow the pressure of life to become greater than the pleasure of life. I feel at times we all are guilty of putting the weight of the world on our shoulders; forgetting that the process is just as important as the outcome. All of us get knocked down, but it's the resiliency that matters. All of us do well when things are going well. But the thing that distinguishes great people from good people is their ability to do well in times of great stress, urgency and pressure.

A knockdown can come from an illness, injury or any other source. We have to know that we can and will recover. While long term goals are important, the short term ones provide the success and opportunities to keep you moving forward. Short term objectives bring immediate focus and direction to your effort.

Expectations, unlike goals, can be more demanding. However, what was won or lost yesterday doesn't really matter. What happened at work, in the classroom, at a ballgame, etc., is ancient history. If you have been disappointed by a loss or a bad day or failing an exam, you can learn from it. Win, lose or fail, we have to move on.

Looking forward is as much about an attitude as it is about not staying stuck in a rut. By looking forward and moving forward, we will get to our goals and accomplish the things in our hearts that we choose to accomplish. So no matter how frustrating or intense our day may become, we can always find a positive experience within it. It's all about how you choose to think; how you choose to see things. The only discipline that lasts is self-discipline. I think that's the steepest part of the learning curve. Why? Because in this world of uncertainty, you are the one thing you can count on.

You must become the producer, director and actor in this unfolding story of your life. No one can depress you, no one can hurt your feelings, no one can make you do anything other than what you allow them to do from the inside. In all honesty, the reality of it is we are human so we will feel pain at times. We will be disappointed at times. Still, each experience in your life is absolutely necessary in order to guide you to that place; to that next level up. So you need to treasure every one of those moments, even the ones you think shouldn't have happened. Every obstacle that comes along in our lives is either an opportunity for us to grow and transcend our form of thinking, our mindsets to think differently or it is an opportunity to use it as a curse to allow us to believe we are stuck in this one particular place for the rest of our lives.

You must understand that your miracles are an inside job. Go there to create the magic that you seek in your life. As they say, 'as a man thinketh in his heart, so is he'. You are the creator of your thoughts. This means in some metaphysical way, you are a co-creator of your life.

Most people are searching for happiness. They are looking for it. They are trying to find it in someone or something outside of themselves. Well, that's a fundamental mistake. Happiness is something that you are and it comes from the way you think. That's why happiness cannot be about other people or things. Think about it. We go to the store and purchase this new car, we are happy. Two, three, four, five, six years later we want another car. We are discontented with this one. So, happiness leaves us. We get happy, and then we purchase something else. That's why happiness is not traced and laced in things.

The difference between a purpose and a goal is that a purpose is ongoing. It can't be achieved. A goal has a beginning and an ending to it which creates that so-called happiness. That's why it's very important we should live our life not goal-driven but purpose-driven. You can accomplish a goal but you can't accomplish your purpose.

You can only continue to work on your purpose. As you are working on your purpose, that work creates personal excellence. Personal excellence is open to everyone.

Let's not become complacent or lazy. Laziness grows on people. Do what has to be done as well as it can be done. In order to succeed greatly, you have to sacrifice greatly. Yes, everything starts with a dream. But without hard work, you may end up with nothing but a dream. Greatness, in its last analysis, is largely commitment and courage embracing high standards and divine principles with a respectable way of doing things. If you do not dare to be different from your friends, family, associates, etc., you will never be great. To get profit without risk, experience without danger, and reward without work, is as impossible as it is to live without being born.

I firmly believe we are put on this earth to be tested, to be challenged with adversity and to see what we can accomplish. The successful person is the one who continuously faces challenges and problems that life brings and overcomes them all, no matter what the obstacle. So, what's your definition of success? What is your definition of happiness?

I also believe it is important to have a philosophy that gives you the gumption to get up and go—that courage, that motivation to make your dreams come true. You see, the great ones have a philosophy in place. The great ones set a standard for themselves to be the best at what they are doing. The desire to succeed should be vibrating through every fiber of your being. So find the task that will call forth your faith, your courage, your perseverance and your spirit of sacrifice. Also, one must be prepared to suffer during the process. If one isn't prepared to suffer during adversities, I don't really see how he or she can be successful. So, crystallize your goals. Make a plan for achieving them and set yourself a deadline. Then, with supreme confidence, determination and a disregard for obstacles—including other people's criticisms—carry out your plans.

Yes, this is a powerful, compelling process, but in the future you will find legitimacy in day-to-day preparation. Reflecting back on what I said earlier, I cannot believe that the purpose of life is just to be happy. I think that the purpose of life is to be useful, to be responsible, to be honorable and to be compassionate. It is above all to matter, to count, to stand for something and to have made some difference that you leave behind proof that you have lived at all.

Understand that everything is either process driven or relationship driven. Learn to be responsible for your failures and supersede your accomplishments. Success isn't about being the best. Success is the ongoing process of becoming your best self. You can be good or you can be outstanding. But, you can't be both. You weren't born in this world to come in and complain. You were brought forth to be of service and produce. Therefore, we must learn to take life's hardships as personal challenges instead of personal setbacks.

Understanding suffering is an unavoidable aspect of our human pilgrimage; the deepest faith cannot prevent our walk through the valley of the shadow of death. When bad things happen to us, it does not mean that our faith fails. Our faith helps us extract meaning from misery and to make sense out of suffering. Our faith should give us comfort that the Almighty walks with us and will never forsake us.

Any piece of knowledge I acquire today—be it spiritual, secular or educational—increases my value tomorrow. I keep this in my mind as I am working with the youth, because the evidence always looks underdetermined. However, I am always full of hope and faith. Yes, having self-esteem is important. For me, it's okay for me to have self-esteem. Nevertheless, I know to put in work because work breeds confidence.

One last thing concerning longevity. Don't get caught up in currents—current events, current challenges, current fears. Stay committed to your decisions; your goals, but be flexible to your approach. Like an airplane, the same winds of problems that blow against us today, if we press on, will be the same problems that will be beneath us tomorrow.

## Reality

While hindsight is 20/20, nothing is crystal clear when it comes to forecasting the future. However, I was told that the best way to create the future is one day at a time. Unfortunately, on the flip side of that same coin, the result of the lack of effort or the lack of planning or no planning at all will see the disheartening reality of our future unfold right before our eyes.

The realities of our life write the narrative during our life. To some people, life is a series of walls with no doors, no windows and no way out. However, I urgently encourage you to use your imagination. An imagination should be used not to escape from reality, but to help you create your reality. Make no mistake about it, your imagination along with a call to action of self determination giving total effort and a sustained work ethic, even then the odds seem entirely against you, will tilt success in your favor. However, by not doing what is necessary, we are forced to ask ourselves do we want to inherit poverty or possibilities.

Not to sound arrogant or conceited, I want to leave the mark of my will, my signature on important acts that I have touched. This is not the voice of my ego, but of my human spirit rising up declaring that it has something to contribute to the solutions to the problems of my chosen vocation. However, make no mistake about it; what matters is not our successes; but our significance.

This brings me to the point that life never needs us, but we need life. That is why it is so important that we embark upon a life of continuous learning. Education is indoctrination if you embrace it, but it is subjugation if you don't embrace it. Well, why do you say this Maurice? I want you to desperately understand there are two objectives for education. First, there is education for living and second, there is education for making a living. Both are as different as night and day. There are times when life becomes a series of hardships and disappointments and the storm clouds of darkness completely dims our vision and it becomes impossible to see how we are going to make it. We must offset eyesight with insight. Everything that happens to you is either an opportunity for you to grow or an obstacle to keep you from growing. You get to choose.

During the turbulent times in life, stand tall and stand strong. Believe in yourself. Consider the past. Evaluate the present. Create the future. In the process, let's not get so caught up in our feelings. Feelings can ruin our lives, so let's keep thinking, planning, strategizing. Life is all about what you can do, not about what you have done. Therefore, we should learn to view the dilemmas of life as opportunities and the difficulties of life as challenges to our creative skills. We are all skilled. It's easy to come up with reasons why something won't or shouldn't brew, but saying "no" to life is not productive.

People who succeed on the job, at work, at home, and at school are people who believe in the possibilities of life. Most people would agree it's important to get what you want, but it's more important to want what you get. In wanting what you get, we must learn to develop a sense of assertiveness—a desire to do well. A desire to do very well; not just meandering or looking from a mediocre point of view, we have to go back and look back over our life and understand the importance of not just doing something, but doing it well. We should put our best foot forward. That's what this is all about.

Every day is a new beginning which allows for progress and possibilities in the future. It's all about putting forth that effort; making that effort because that's a signature of who you are. Regardless of how badly you want to be successful, you must put yourself in the position to be successful. How do you do that? If one of my goals is to become Mr. America or Mr. USA, I can't spend more time lounging around on the couch than I do in the gym. I can't say I want to be a doctor if I don't have the internal educational fortitude to continue my education. I can't say I want to become a successful writer if I don't partake of learning the English language and learning the importance of being an orator or learn the importance of self expression by way of words.

## Conclusion: Success

Finally we come to Success. Success is the result of hard work and learning from failure.

Here is my prescription for work: If your health is threatened—work. If disappointments come—work. If your faith falters—work. If your dreams are shattered and your hopes begin to fade—work. If sorrow overwhelms you—work. If your friends prove untrue and desert you---work. Get busy and work with all your might. There is no such thing as failure for the willing, ambitious worker.

Conditions are never just right. People who delay actions until all factors are favorable do nothing. People do not decide their future; they decide their habits and their habits decide their future. During the process, sometimes you have to reboot and set your mind for the difficult tasks ahead. Remember, if you are still alive, your mission on Earth is never finished. Even through the ups and downs, a successful man is one who can lay a firm foundation with the bricks that others and life has thrown at him. The better you become, the more people will try to find something wrong with you.

Too often, progress has been delayed or even halted by people who use the word impossible. Well, transplant a human heart—impossible. Put a man on the moon—impossible. Elect a black man as President of the USA—impossible. Over time, the impossible becomes possible. These are only tests of our ingenuity as humans.

As I finally come to an end, I would like to bring forth what I call the 4 L's: live, learn, love and leave a legacy.

- Live and not just exist. Enjoy and appreciate life for what it is.
- Learn, because the more you learn, the better you feel about yourself and the more productive you will become.
- Love, love is the most powerful force on earth! How we use it will determine how high up we will go in our life.
- Leave a legacy. Leave a positive imprint on the world that will touch and help change the lives of others through your works and accomplishments.

Thank you.

Connect with Maurice on Facebook!
www.facebook.com/Maurice-Blair-869839526464002/

Notes ~~~ Looking at some of *Maurice's Mile Markers of Life* below, reflect on them and write down what they may mean for you.

1. "Any adversity you faced and overcame throughout your life has prepared you for this moment in time." What adversity has made you better?

   _____
   _____
   _____
   _____
   _____
   _____

2. "To succeed or even to survive these days demands an unending attention to detail." I know this to be true because:

   _____
   _____
   _____
   _____
   _____
   _____

3. "Complacency can sabotage your job, your health and your family." Three (3) ways I can end complacency and stay curious in my life include:

   _____
   _____
   _____
   _____
   _____
   _____

4. "Security never comes from contracts or employment arrangements; it comes from ability, skill and dedication." I have the ability to _____, the skills for _____, and I show my dedication by _____
   _____.

5. "Not everyone can go to college, but everyone can be educated." I am educated in _____ _____.

6. "There is no such thing as try power; it's will power. Will power is the power to choose." I know the difference because

   _____
   _____
   _____
   _____
   _____

7. "Truly successful people are always reaching and stretching." I could reach and stretch right now to be successful at

   _____
   _____. I will reach and stretch by
   _____
   _____
   _____
   _____
   _____

8. "It's a funny thing how people doubt their beliefs and believe their doubts." The last time I believed my doubts I lost an opportunity to

   _____
   _____
   _____
   _____
   _____

9. "Having character is much more important than being a "character." When I HAVE character I behave in ways that

   _____
   _____
   _____

_____
_____

10. "Even in the most impossible situations, stand tall and keep your head up, shoulders back; keep moving, running, looking up demonstrating your pride, dignity and defiance." I have pride in my _____' I express my dignity by _____. I defy failure by _____ _____.

Notes~~~

www.ingramcontent.com/pod-product-compliance
Lightning Source LLC
Chambersburg PA
CBHW060427050426
42449CB00009B/2167